charles brunet

worth and divine

LOSTPRESS

ISBN 978-1-7752974-5-1

http://charlesantoinebrunet.wixsite.com/lostpress

First Edition.

girl,
you were thicker than a
bowl of oatmeal
but you weren't
        gluten

              free

           -itsdivya

contents

a.

On the ground

There i am

Am i worthy now?

worth and divine

It's not what is said about you that
matters
But more what is thought by you
You are more than what others say you are

People in the subway
      You know their songs are good
In their headphones
              Because they act as if
                   They are
In a music video

worth and divine

If an elephant walked in right now
In the middle of our kiss
                        Right now
Would you even notice?
            Or are you too preoccupied by your own
                                    Desires

To witness what is happening around you
                        ?

9

Enough.
Time is slow right now
But enough
It is now that i need to be
                    Breathe
Slowly. I become.

They say boys are wild
                    And we are
                        In a way
But we also do have hearts
Contrary to popular belief

Don't let the others tell you things
Don't generalize
Before you have made your mind
            On
                Your
                    Own

My grey shirt is torn
By claws inside my chest.

I am a devil whose horns you cut off.

I would like to apologize
To all the people i have hurt in
My passage through their
                    Existences
You were not meant to stay.
I was meant to leave.

And for that
                    I am sorry.

worth and divine

I forgot how to be myself because of
you
And yet because of you i became more like
me

I wish i could be a witch
Because witches make potions
I could make a love potion
                    Make you love me
But i cannot
You cannot
And so instead i write poems

I feel your soft breath against my spine
Oh how my back hurts because of you
Your hollow
You hollow

Don't leave me hanging like a fly on your wall

I will hear everything

We were having a meaningless conversation
So i left

I feel better now

You said you wanted to go to brazil
I didn't want to go to brazil
It's too hot and lonely
Too intense
I wanted to stay home

You went to brazil
You never came back

I should have left with you
When you begged me
Now i want to open
                    My window
        And scream your name
But you won't hear a thing
You never did anyway

worth and divine

This morning there was blood on the sink
It was red
            Crimson
It felt strange in my mouth
It felt alien
            I am alienated
                        It smelled of tar
                        And of bones
            I am alienated

31

b.

There were three boys
And
Three girls

But none wanted to be there
Yet they stayed
They strayed

        Honest mistake, i guess

My clothes smell like a fire
I do not smell like they do
I smell fine
Like jewelry
Like
Gold

My house was flooded
The fire extinguished
Yet the gold remains
like
Photographs in black and white

Once
Upon
A
Time
A
Boy
Wanted
To
Be
A
Prince

But
Princes
Have
Feelings
Which
Is
Not
Allowed
For
Real
Little
Boys

worth and divine

And
Once
Upon
A
Time
The
Boy
Became
A
Prince
Nonetheless
And

Was
Shunned
By
All
The
Other
Boys
Because
Of
The
Feelings
He
Expressed
Through
Art
And
Words

Boys can be mean
They can be cruel
          But it is not the boys that are to be blamed
                              It is their parents
                    And their lack of parenting

And socicty
Which does not let people be who
          They
                    Truly
     Are

I used to like you
But then i changed
And i realized i don't need you
And i don't wanna be you anymore

If a reader
Loses his place in a book
He loses his identity
This happened multiple times

This happens still to this day

Let the others give you value
If you need to
But first
Discover your worth
Discover yourself
So that you know
What
You
Truly
Deserve

worth and divine

You said we were all the same
But
                        In the end
We were not.

            Only opposites

I am similar to a video you
would play on the background
As white noise
To fill your head
Erase anything else
But i am more
I am human
Or at least i think

worth and divine

Silence
Don't think
Don't breathe
Silence
silence

Was i nothing
But
A chapter
To you?

I do not miss you
If that's what you were wondering
But i do wonder
About why
You abandoned me so quickly

worth and divine

The sky is with me tonight
Like
      It is with me in my mind
              On my mind,
                In my eyes
In yours, too
But don't be mistaken
      Nothing of this is forever

Sometimes i wonder
If you understand time like i do

If it means what
                    It does
            For me

Because you throw away your life
Like it does not mean
                    Anything

Tonight i drank an entire
Bottle
It was white
It was sweet
It makes me feel fuzzy
It makes me feel what no feelings
Feel   like
And it is sweet
So so sweet

Now
The
Forest
Feels
Softer
Like
Its
Light
Has
Been
Dimmed
And
To
Be
Honest
I
Like
It
Because
It
Makes
Me
Feel
Better
About
My
Inner
Darkness

There should be more to this
A distant but still close
Shoulder
A leftover bone to chew on
Something more
Something left of us

But you burned it all with your mind

You unplugged my computer
Severed it from its cord
Like you did to me
Severed me from your heart

I hope it didn't hurt you as much as it hurt it

worth and divine

You brought the sun

Because of you
We had a nice weekend

worth and divine

Are you gonna judge me like
God?

                        No no no i
            Don't think   so

You honked at me like
I was a cute mcdonalds girl

But i'm a 20 year old man

You need glasses

Candles with flames are burning
And i can feel their heat
Because even though you made
it into my mind again

I know i deserve better

Listen to the trees
The wind
The fires
The rain pouring

Listen

No one else can do it like you do

I feel like music
Should be thought of as more important

And that anyone
Should be allowed to have a song

Repeat after me

I am not the sum of all my parts
I am much much more

I deserve every thing

Breathe
Inhale
Exhale
Close your eyes
Sleep
It'll be better
When you've allowed
Yourself
To rest

The fall will eventually come back
And so will i
In another form perhaps

Unoriginal is the new pretty
They say

And we all know i can be
                        both

this book was created within 24 hours
as a part of the rk project.

Special thanks to all instagram poets and various other
inspirations that helped carry out this collection.